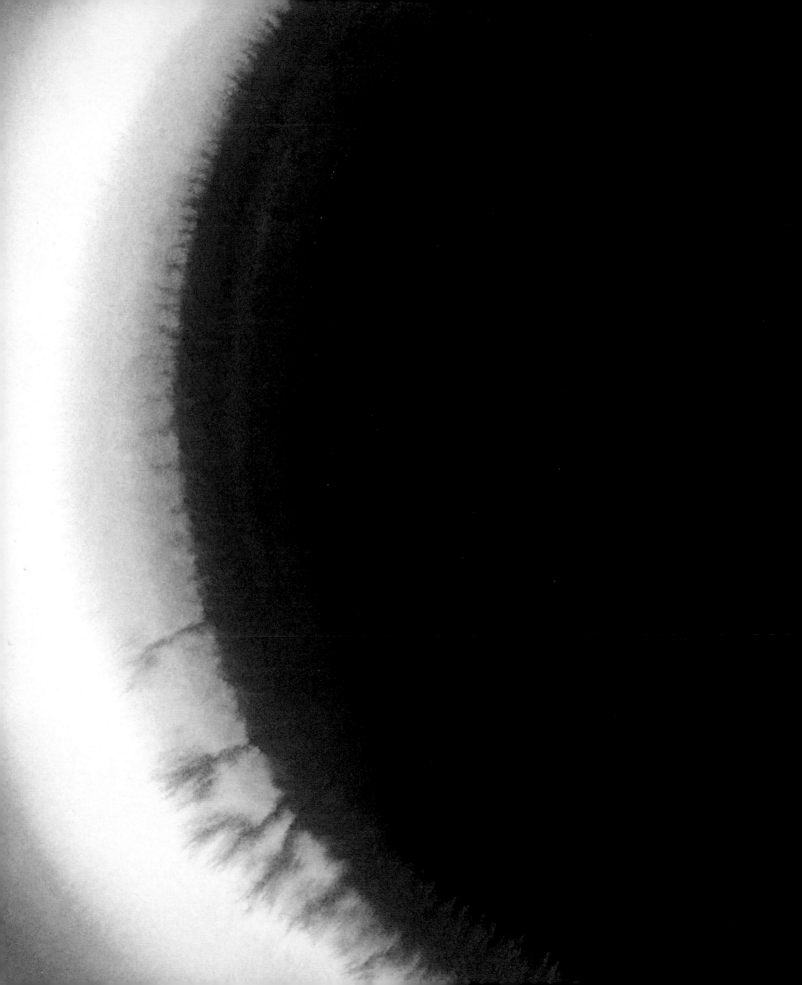

Meet the Universe

I'm a BLACK HOLE

DR. EVE M. VAVAGIAKIS

ILLUSTRATED BY JESSICA LANAN

mit Kids Press

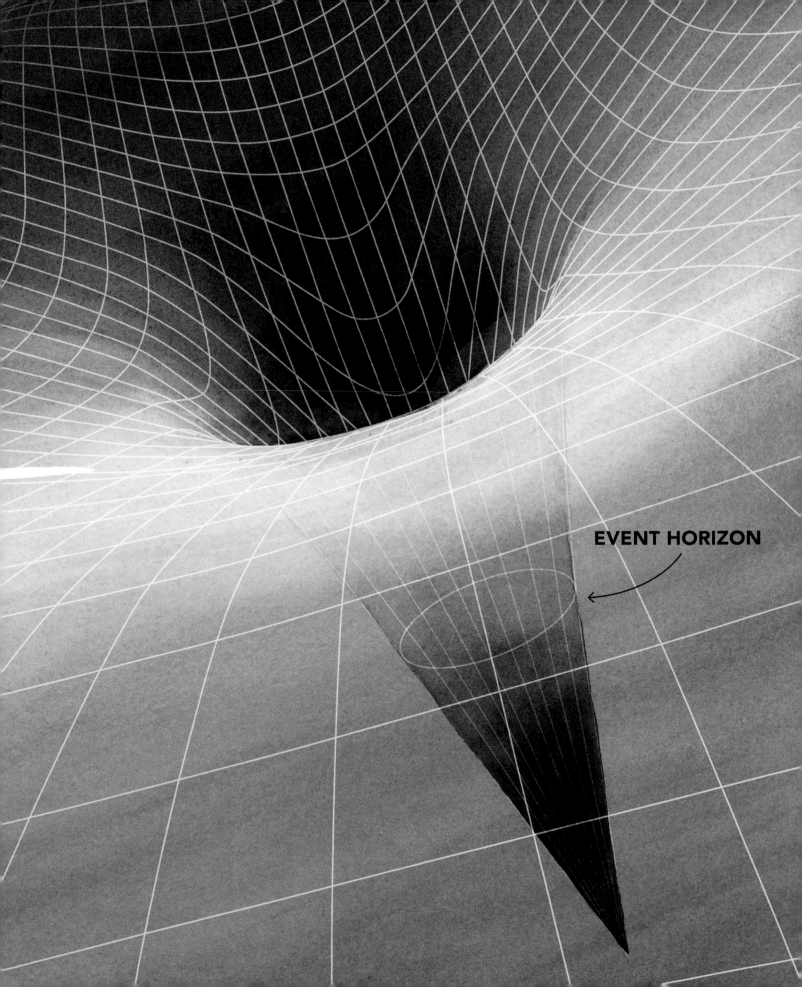

EVENT HORIZON

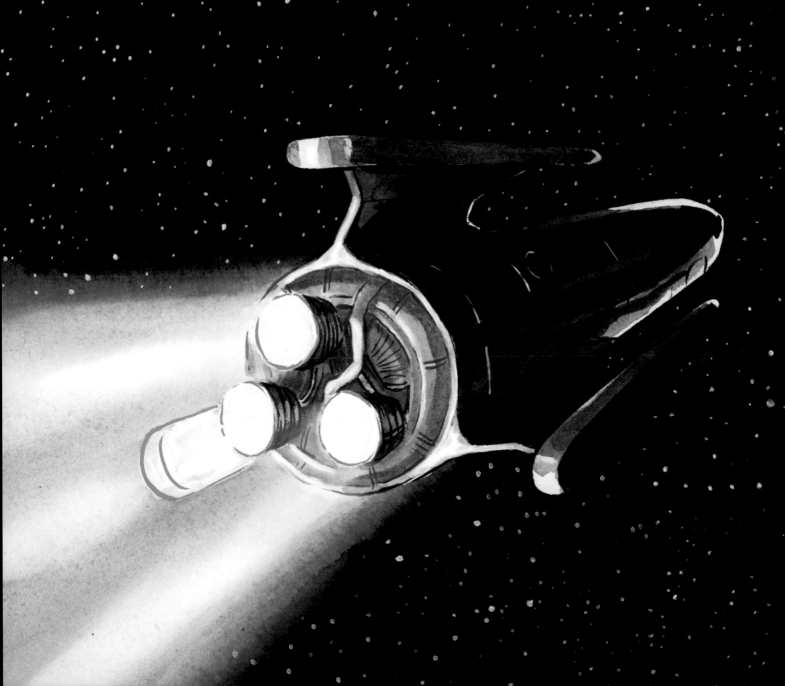

I remain hidden where I live out in space.
You can't see me directly. I can be hard to trace.

I was made from a star
much bigger than the sun.
When that huge star collapsed,
my life had begun.

I grew and I grew, eating up what passed by.
I pulled in stars, planets, moons—anything in the sky!

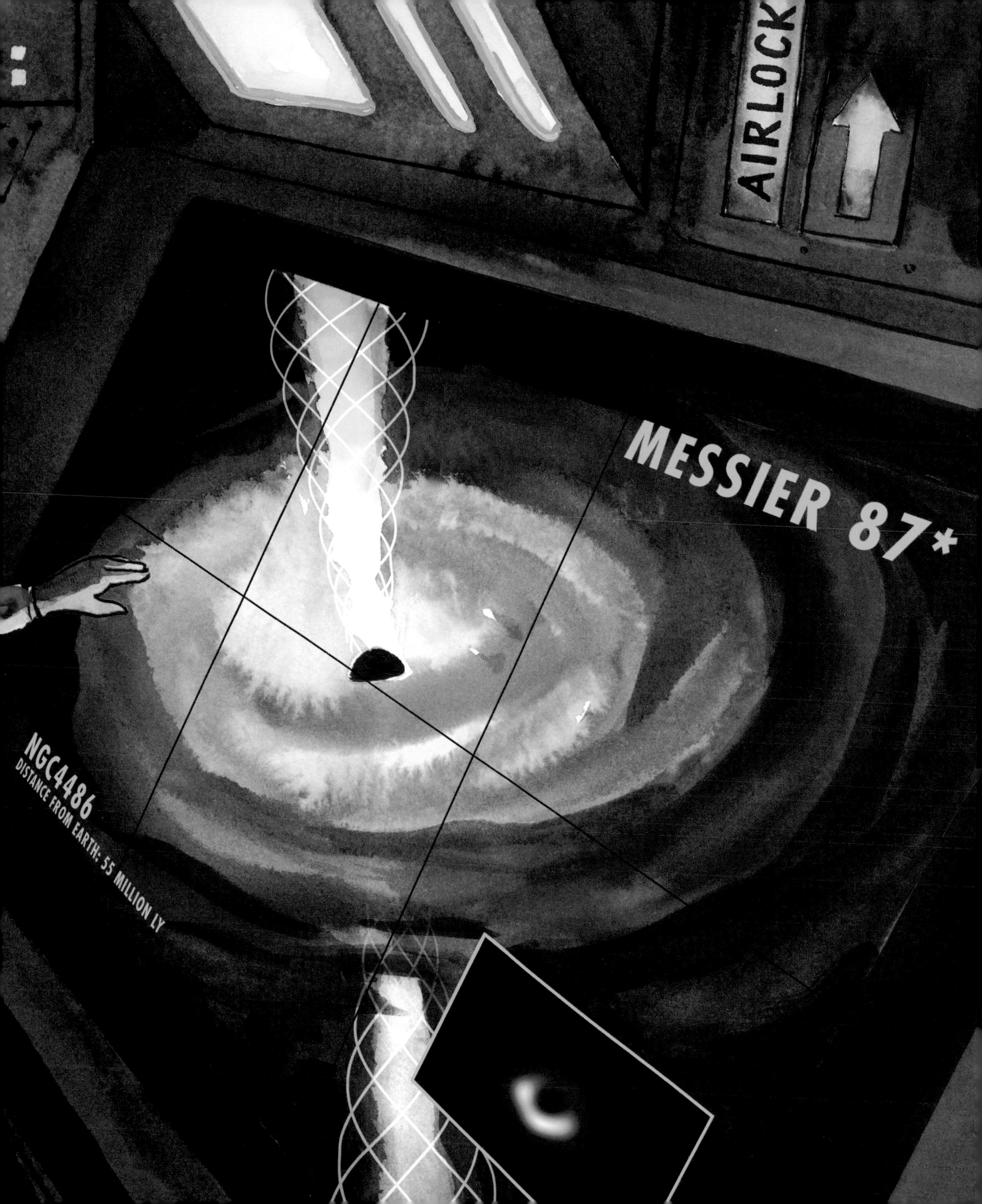
AIRLOCK
MESSIER 87*
NGC4486
DISTANCE FROM EARTH: 55 MILLION LY

Even other black holes! And I am not done: soon I will weigh more than a million suns.

I'm a mysterious object, and I like it that way,
making physicists work hard to understand me today.

I still hold my secrets—physicists wish they knew.
Who will find out? Will it one day be you?

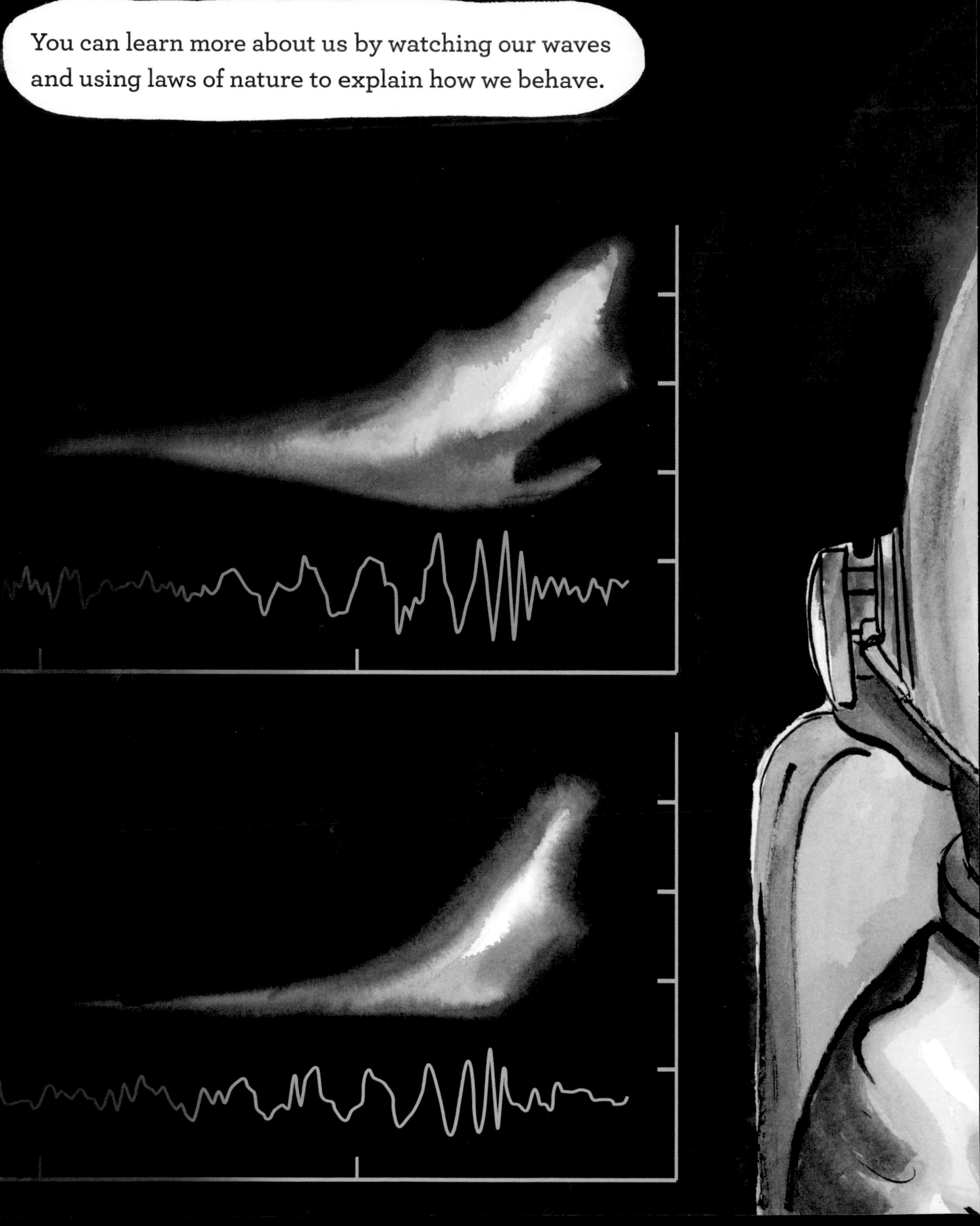
You can learn more about us by watching our waves and using laws of nature to explain how we behave.

When I meet more black holes that are as dense as can be, we make waves in space-time, ripples in gravity!

So when you look at the sky, you will know that I'm there, pulling in anything: light, dust, rocks, or air.

KNOW YOUR BLACK HOLES

A black hole is an object in space that has so much mass in such a small radius that nothing can escape that radius. The mass of an object tells us how much matter or energy it contains, and the weight of an object measures the force of gravity pulling on it. A black hole contains a lot of energy in a very small space.

Just as Earth's gravitational pull keeps us on the ground, the gravitational pull of a black hole can keep matter inside of it. The pull is strong enough that even light can get trapped inside. This is because a black hole is so compact, meaning it contains a lot of energy in a very small space.

Don't worry—you won't get trapped by a black hole because you will not be close enough to one. Matter won't get swallowed up by a black hole unless it gets too close. The event horizon of a black hole is the boundary in space around the black hole past which nothing can escape, not even light! If a black hole had the same mass as Earth, its event horizon would have a radius of less than an inch. That's smaller than a Ping-Pong ball!

Because we can't measure any light coming from black holes, we can't see them directly! We need to use other tools to learn about black holes. For example, scientists can see how a black hole's gravity affects the surrounding stars and gas. Matter heats up and glows when it gets close to a black hole. Scientists can study the light from this glow. Black holes also warp space such that light bends around the black hole before getting to us here on Earth. This bending of light can produce a lensed effect, known as an Einstein ring.

Some black holes formed from stars. Once the stars ran out of fuel to burn, their gravitational pull overcame their internal pressure and they collapsed. Only a very massive star can be dense enough when it collapses to form a black hole.

Black holes grow in mass by pulling in the matter around them. They're not picky; anything that gets too close to the black hole will be trapped. If they are far enough away, objects can orbit a black hole without falling in. Black holes will not suck in objects like a vacuum cleaner. If our sun were replaced with a black hole of the same mass, for example, Earth's orbit would not change.

Black holes can also combine with other black holes. When black holes collide and merge, they release large amounts of energy. These collisions send gravitational waves through the universe that we can sometimes measure on Earth. The biggest black holes are supermassive black holes, which can weigh millions or billions of times more than our sun.

Many questions about black holes remain to be answered. We don't know exactly what happens inside black holes or how they interact with the matter in our universe. Scientists are working on experiments and theories to explain how black holes behave.

The first image ever captured of a black hole was published by the Event Horizon Telescope Collaboration on April 10, 2019. This black hole lies at the center of a galaxy named Messier 87, and it is billions of times more massive than our sun. When we learn more about black holes, we'll understand more about the physical laws that govern nature. Could you help solve this puzzle by studying black holes?

When black holes get close to each other, a dance starts! They orbit each other, getting closer and closer. This makes gravitational waves: ripples in the fabric of space-time itself. The first observation of gravitational waves was made on September 14, 2015, by the LIGO and Virgo collaborations. In 2017, the Nobel Prize in Physics was awarded to Rainer Weiss, Barry Barish, and Kip Thorne "for decisive contributions to the LIGO detector and the observation of gravitational waves."

Gravitational waves can travel very long distances. We can't watch the black holes as they dance, but we can measure these ripples and use them to learn about the properties of the black holes. Other objects can also be studied using gravitational waves, including merging and exploding stars.

Many scientists are currently investigating black holes. Some scientists are using the Chandra X-ray Observatory, a telescope out in space, to take measurements of X-rays produced from matter close to black holes. These measurements are teaching us about where black holes can exist and how they behave.

When black holes grow in mass, they accelerate matter near them. This matter can propel particles away from the black hole close to the speed of light in huge beams called jets. We can observe these bright and energetic jets with our telescopes.

Black holes are everywhere! In 2020, Reinhard Genzel and Andrea Ghez were awarded the Nobel Prize in Physics for their discovery that a supermassive object called Sagittarius A*, millions of times more massive than our own sun, can only be explained as a black hole. On May 12, 2022, the Event Horizon Telescope Collaboration released the first image of material around the horizon of Sagittarius A*, confirming it to be a black hole. Evidence also suggests thousands of smaller black holes lie near the center of our galaxy.

When you look up into the night sky, it's amazing to think about all the black holes in our universe dancing with one another, making ripples in space, and eating up lots of matter! Black holes will live on for an extremely long time, much longer than the amount of time our universe has existed.

FOR FURTHER EXPLORATION

Check out the websites below to learn more about the science in this book.

On black holes: https://www.nasa.gov/black-holes

On the Event Horizon Telescope: https://eventhorizontelescope.org

On LIGO: https://www.ligo.org/science.php

On the Chandra X-ray Observatory: https://chandra.harvard.edu

On the Nobel Prize: https://nobelprize.org

*To my cousins, big and little, and everyone who takes courageous
steps into the unknown*
EMV

For Abbie, who kept me safely on this side of the event horizon
JL

The MIT Press, the ☰**mit Kids** Press colophon, and MIT Kids Press are
trademarks of The MIT Press, a department of the Massachusetts Institute of
Technology, and used under license from The MIT Press. The colophon and
MIT Kids Press are registered in the US Patent and Trademark Office.

First edition 2024

Library of Congress Catalog Card Number pending
ISBN 978-1-5362-2208-1

23 24 25 26 27 28 APS 10 9 8 7 6 5 4 3 2 1

Printed in Humen, Dongguan, China

This book was typeset in Archer.
The illustrations were done in watercolor, ink, gouache, and digital collage.

MIT Kids Press
an imprint of Candlewick Press
99 Dover Street
Somerville, Massachusetts 02144

mitkidspress.com
candlewick.com